Essay, Essay, Essay

The Overseas Memoirs

of

Yasuo Kobachi

Savant Books
Honolulu, Hawaii, USA
2013

Published in the USA by Savant Books
2630 Kapiolani Blvd #1601
Honolulu, HI 96826 USA

Cover Design by Daniel S. Janik
Front Cover Photos by Yasuo Kobachi
Interior Artworks by Kashu Kobachi
Author Photo by Michiko Kobachi
Back Cover Photo by Daniel S. Janik

Second Edition 2013
First Edition (Savant 2008)

ISBN: 9780985250669

Dedication

For my white-haired parents,

Michiko and Mitsuzo Kobachi

- Yasuo Kobachi

Acknowledgment

I want to sincerely thank Dr. Daniel S. Janik and also the instructors and my classmates at Intercultural Communications College (ICC) in Honolulu, Hawaii, USA, as well as the many Americans I have met.

Forward

I have been lucky enough to enjoy studying in Hawaii and am happy to publish this first collection of essays based on my study of American essay writing.

Table of Contents

Y. Kobachi

Torii - A Sacred Arch at the Shrine

1
Who Would I Be?

For a Japanese visitor to Hawaii, one of the most significant and enduring experiences possible has to include becoming a one-day-Shinto-priest. Shinto, the oldest of Japan's religions, has its roots in ancient pantheism in a time when all objects, animate or inanimate, had a soul. The Izumo Taishakyo Mission of Hawaii, or simply Izumo Taisha, a Shinto shrine associated with Japan's second most important shrine after Ise Jingu, has served the Japanese community in Hawaii for over 100 years.

One glorious morning in late fall, before classes, a visiting professor from Japan, Atsushi, holding a list of volunteers, asked, "Yasu, do you plan to participate in the the New Year's holiday?"

At that very moment, I was just beginning to doze off and responded without thinking, "Sure, but what would I be able to do at the shrine?"

He bluntly told me, "You're going to be dressed in priest's clothing, and be a priest!"

I was totally stunned and mumbled to him, "Huh? I'm going be…? No way! You're putting me on!"

"Actually, I'm not," he replied. "The New Year Holiday Planning Committee will hold a briefing, an explanatory meeting, at five o'clock in the evening on December twenty-second. I'll see you there." That was that.

On the fateful day, I went to the meeting only to discover how small the shine appeared compared to the original in Japan, where I had paid a visit some years before. As a matter of fact, the shrine in Japan, the largest wooden building in the world, has endured for centuries. I strolled around and met the other New Year volunteers.   Eventually, Rev. Amano, whom I had already been acquainted with, started to explain the Shinto ideas of charms, altars, and clothes: what they mean, what happiness or virtue each brings, and how to wear the sacred clothes. Afterwards, everyone went for dinner in Chinatown and then parted, some like me taking a bus home, while others, the alcohol addicts, grabbed a cab to a local bar for a drink.

On New Year's Day, I arrived early and asked Rev. Amano what I should do. It was early morning, and the constant drizzle and gusting winds went contrary to our hope and expectations.   Following Rev. Amano's explicit instructions, I solemnly dressed in priest robes, and stood, shaking my "gohei," a tool to purify and give people a New Year's blessing, all the while quietly chanting the short Shinto prayer he had taught me. It took much longer for the people to worship than I expected, though there appeared to be no long line.

At first I didn't feel right, but I quickly got used to my new role. After some time passed, I was relieved by another "priest" and began watching the visitors, mainly third or fourth generation Japanese-Americans. On the whole, they seemed to have forgotten the details of the Japanese traditions and customs. Resuming my priestly role, I noticed that some appeared to worship me rather than the god behind me, and others asked me how to worship. For example, several asked how many times to clap their hands, an important part of the ceremony in which one wakes up the gods so they will notice us. Rev. Amano came to my aid: "Four times is correct in this shrine; however, even twice is alright."

As the evening progressed, I found myself bonding with the worshippers, feeling something intangible inside about their attitude, and in their coming to know something more about their roots, deep down in their hearts re-identifying with the ancient Japan from where they came.

When I later e-mailed this story to a friend, he replied jokingly that most people would be pleased to have a happy, safe and prosperous new year, even if blessed by a "fake" priest. But, indeed, as I think about it, I have had just such a new year. That is, however, a story for another time.

You Look Familiar

2

The Sphinx for Our Times

With a startled look, the Sphinx silently greets everyone. Her physical appearance awakes old memories of Sesame Street, though she never appears on it. She has zillions of live friends of the same species all over the world. After the devastating "avian flu outbreak," millions of her friends ended up in the garbage. Each year, billions of her endearing friends in every country sacrifice their lives for human beings. However, this particular Sphinx lives in a fantasy world catering mainly to children and teenage girls. So, roll out the red carpet for the mystery woman of today.

This regal lady stands one foot two inches tall. She sports three-and-a-half-inch folded triangular wings which become 11 inches across when outstretched. People giggle at her oval head, strong neck, sturdy tail and dumpy body with a beautifully pear-shaped waistline that makes her look like a round 25 ounce whisky bottle. Her tail measures two inches long by three inches wide and has a one-inch-wide, flaring orange stripe at the edge. Her short one-inch legs go well with her two-inch wide, webbed feet. Her gaudy legs and feet flash with alternating whitish orange and black horizontal stripes. Her body, clad head to tail in half-inch golden brown and satin tan feathers, sports a shiny flaming-orange tail.

What makes this chick so special? Perhaps her big, jaunty, yellowish orange beak made of soft fleece symbolizes her character. This beauty, however, also flaunts a sporty crimson-red comb and wattle, and around her neck, a matching crimson-red scarf that makes her look a bit cow-girlish. Her wide white plastic eyes and big black pupils charm everyone who looks at her, though she stares blankly forward.

Though she looks soft all over, she has heavy-duty plastic bones in her beak, neck, wings, tail, legs and body. Her crest, wattle, scarf and beak, however, feel velvety smooth.

A selector switch ("on," "off" or "auto") is built into her black bottom, and guess what happens when one turns it "on" or switches it over to "auto?" Though she weighs a little over one pound and, unlike the same species in the real world, can neither fly nor hop, she begins to flap around to a rasping, up-tempo march, occasionally stopping to clamor out in a hoarse singing voice a "cluck-cluck" while fluttering her wings stiffly.

A ball-point pen tapped on her plastic eyes makes a dull click. Tapping on her body creates a muffled sound. This mannequin lady smells of new sofa fabric with a hint of human odor.

Nobody would savor eating this Sphinx. However, her tasty real-life friends appear on millions of people's dinner tables every day throughout the world.

So, do you, dear reader, have a guess as to what or who she is?

A Small Present for You

3

A Tip for a Tip

The definition of the noun, "tip," in the dictionary portion of Dictionary.com reads, "a small present of money given directly to someone for performing a service or menial task; gratuity: He gave the waiter a dollar as a tip." The noun, "service," on the other hand, means, "an act of helpful activity; help; aid: to do someone a service." Combining these two definitions, one could redefine the meaning of "tip" as follows; "a small present of money given directly to someone for performing a helpful activity, providing help or aid, or doing menial work."

When the television news two years ago reported that servers at fancy restaurants in New York City earned a much higher income than cooks, Yasu, an international student at Intercultural Communications College (ICC) in Honolulu, Hawaii, and his parents, with an amazed look, simply uttered, "Oh boy! What a bunch of nonsense!" After a brief pause, the parents shrugged their shoulders and continued, "Well, anything can happen in America."

Yasu, however, replied, "Wait! It doesn't make sense. Servers make more money than cooks? They're wagging the dog instead of the tail!" Did New Yorkers really value good service more than excellent food? Wake up and smell the coffee, Americans! The time has come to ban tipping, an absurd practice which has turned into an incomprehensible, social rule that Americans have somehow iconized into "etiquette."

Tipping made its debut long ago in America. James Surowiecki on a website entitled "The New Yorker" in the second paragraph reports, "Tipping didn't take hold here until after the Civil War." Yasu wondered if since then, Americans have cherished the tipping custom in order to create a whole new culture to cover up the lack thereof. To him, it remains difficult to conceptualize a country that waged war against Great Britain so as to free its colonists from double paying, which can't kick such an irrational habit. Do freedom loving Americans secretly desire the return of antiquated, aristocratic master-servant relations in the New World? Unlikely. Perhaps they're just getting complacent about "tipping the servants?" Actually, Americans do not need to retain any such vestige of un-American Old World patronage.

Management, not the customer should have to figure out how much to charge to serve a meal and provide workers with a decent income. .On ThinkandAsk.com, paragraph seven explicitly states: "fault your management for your poor wage. Your salary is not the responsibility of your customers." The author of this essay couldn't agree more. Customers should not have to hire the serving staff, and visitors or travelers surely shouldn't have to worry about workers' wages. Management needs to put the horses before the cart.

Every tipped worker should stand up for his or her right to live a stable, self-supporting life. Angela Dilanzo, a Tour Manager in the USA of Contiki.com, explains in her article, "Tipping – North America," that workers such as waiters, bartenders, delivery people, taxi cab drivers, bathroom attendants, hairstylists, and manicurists receive hourly rates as low as $2.83 an hour. If these tipped workers can't live in comfort working at this hourly rate, then they should appeal to the United States government to increase the minimum wage, or to management to raise their wages, or simply go on strike. Usually customers, often tipped workers also, will support their demands.

Tips are difficult to calculate. According to article 4.4 of "Tipping by Region" in Wikipedia, The Free Encyclopedia, working Americans expect different tip amounts under different circumstances. Visitors, tourists and Americans unfamiliar with this social institution have to take a list with them wherever they go in order to meet worker needs and expectations. Why in the world should a customer have to bother to memorize each worker's particular business and tipping scale? According to ICC's English 101 instructor, Dr. Daniel S. Janik, educated Americans appreciate clearness, conciseness, and completeness. Just imagine life with no annoying tipping calculations. American consumers need to jettison this awful social act that alone can wet-blanket an otherwise enjoyable dinner.

Tipping habits are actually tantamount to tactical tax evasion. Preying on its customers, the hospitality industry employs lower wage workers forcing them to depend on this bizarre customary practice. In this sense, encouraging or participating in tipping becomes a premeditated form of illegal tax evasion. American people should rethink this practice that only the criminal few can feel happy about.

When one catches a cab and the driver asks for a tip, this can not constitute "an act of helpful activity" in any sense of the word. Taking a customer to a mutually agreed-upon destination does not qualify as an "additional service." It simply is the service. People don't give a money present to a commercial airline pilot when they arrive at their expected destination. Isn't it time to get rid of this gravy train that, in the end, benefits no one?

Summing up, America needs to ban tipping. Rational Americans should not look on this custom as "etiquette," but rather as an archaic albatross hanging heavily and awkwardly about their nation's neck.

Need Help?

4

Paradise on Earth

When the author, an international student from Japan, first walked through United States customs at Honolulu International Airport, he stopped, amazed at the many different shades of skin color in the crowd greeting him. To his even greater astonishment, when he hailed a taxi, an unnecessarily long stretch limo pulled up and the driver showed him a rate schedule, speaking quickly to him not in English but some other distinctly unAmerican language!

Riding through Honolulu, he marveled at the city's organization. Honolulu seemed roomier, and the streets more spacious and uncrowded than his Japanese hometown. In Waikiki, wherever he strolled, every street had a given name, greatly facilitating access by guests and newly-arrived foreigners to any desired place. Almost every street had green trees that pleasantly shielded walkers from the glaring midday sun.

The shops along the road displayed only appropriate advertisements; no billboards shouted garishly, tempting passersby to indulge in questionable behavior. Instead, signs caught his eye mainly by virtue of their surprisingly non-English characters. Moreover, public parking lots, restrooms, and water coolers comfortably accommodated thousands of people all enjoying a variety of marine sports, as well as outdoor picnics and barbecues. People could use these facilities for free only needing to heed a few strict laws, like no alcohol on the beach. To his delight, no matter how hard he searched, he could find no trash or bits of hazardous broken glass scattered on the beaches or lawns. Truly, he had stumbled into paradise!

When he caught a bus, the driver gave him a transfer ticket that enabled him to ride another bus which took him back to where he first got on, all for only two dollars! Everything about the bus, even the passengers showed respect for the physically challenged; the bus, for example, when stopping, often kneeled down politely and extended a platform out to help them. Local youths riding the bus, though shivering in the chill wind constantly belching out of the bus air conditioner, willingly gave up their seats to the elderly.

Whenever he needed a hand, citizens always had a courteous reply, never giving him the cold shoulder. When he was lost, residents gladly explained or pointed out the way for him, even if they didn't know for sure. In fact, despite being a stranger, he never once felt uncomfortable, even though he did not have command of spoken English and spoke with a distinctly Japanese accent. "Locals" always smiled at him when their eyes met, even though they didn't know him. People in Hawaii constantly showed their famous Aloha Spirit.

When he ate out at a restaurant, he always received a free glass of delightfully pure Hawaiian water. As he drank, he thanked the tap water goddess, the Honolulu Board of Water Supply, for not adding dangerous, smelly chlorine to the pure Hawaiian water which so agreed with him. Thinking suddenly of the misty, rain-forested mountains, he marveled that in spite of all the humans on the little island, the water seemed, like their Aloha Sprit, unlimited.

At first, when he ordered food, the large potions overwhelmed him, quickly helping unravel for him the riddle of the American "doggy bag," an initially perplexing custom since he had left his pet dog at home in Japan. When he asked for the check, he found tipping, a worrisome non-Japanese custom, surprisingly easy. In spite of his reservations, it gave him a good feeling, he decided, to reward extra service.

When he entered a friend's house, he paused to take off his shoes at the door, but was instead waved inside. All the time he and his friends talked, the TV blared. The commercials, loud and demanding, seemed to last forever. When the weather forecast for Hawaii finally appeared, he thought meteorologists here surely had an easy job because even he could predict with assurance the "mostly sunny" all year round. When he looked out a window into the sky, he felt he would never again know such magically extravagant and brilliant weather as in Hawaii. Throughout his stay in Hawaii, he would often write to his friend in southern England, "Eat your heart out!"

Before he knew it, all his allergic woes had left him. He no longer suffered from the red, itchy, watery eyes, constant runny nose and sneezing so often alluded to on the television commercials. He quietly thanked the gods and goddesses of Hawaii acknowledging his great debt of gratitude to them.

When later he decided to purchase a used car, the prices took his breath away. Even a "surfer special," a lemon by most country's standards, carried a huge price tag, leaving him dazed. However, once negotiated and purchased, he enjoyed driving his "island car" and further exploring the island. Interestingly, he found he could turn right at most intersections, even when the light beamed red and felt very impressed with such the logical laws, though admittedly they sometimes differed from signal to signal.

Almost every driver in Hawaii kindly let him cut in front of them when necessary. When he took the main freeway, referred to in Hawaii as "H1" to distinguish it from the only other two freeways on the island, he liked not having to pay a toll, which left him with more money in his pocket but admittedly feeling a little guilty when remembering the many expensive expressways in his country. Hawaii drivers, he found out later, still paid a toll, but in repairs from the deep potholes that seemed to lurk everywhere on the island just waiting for him to try to pass by.

Early in the morning, he awoke to loud noises of working people. People in Hawaii, he learned, worked hard, usually at more than one job, just to make ends meet.

When later he decided to look around at open houses one Sunday, he was shocked to find that even a dilapidated, half-century-old derelict could cost a million dollars or more. Suddenly, as he gladly paid his rent, he thought of the thousands of homeless Hawaiians and many cases of petty theft in Hawai, attributing them to Hawaii's outrageous economy.

Clearly, only the wildly rich could live here and own a house.

At ICC, as he studied American English, his teachers relentlessly corrected him, especially whenever he spoke Pidgin English, Hapa (part) Hawaiian or any of the tens of international combinations of English and local dialects. How many languages would one need in addition to English to live and work in Hawai, he wondered? Sometimes, for example, sitting in a restaurant, he heard American English spoken so rarely he would wonder what country he was visiting. Even so, as the weeks slipped by, he came to enjoy his life in what truly deserved the nickname of the Rainbow State.

She is Smiling at Me

5

A Dog's Life

As one might guess, people keep a variety of domestic animals as pets or for commercial purposes. However, dogs make a unique contribution to humanity. These friendly helpmates often give comfort and help alleviate serious patients' woes and burdens. They also make lifelong friends and sometimes act as servants. In short, dogs are easily the most important animal in my home country, Japan.

A friend of mine in Himeji city, Ken Umeda, who loves living creatures, works for Guide Dogs for the Blind (GDB). He always admired GDB dogs' perseverance and intelligence and often claimed, "There's no match for well-trained dogs in supporting human life." In fact, men's best friends can become so devoted to their human partners, as in the case of a seeing-eye dog and its blind partner, that they will gladly serve the person throughout their whole life. For the blind or weak-sighted, such service dogs become the best friend and colleague they could ever have.

Secondly, Japan has quite a large number of elders for whom dogs are special. According to tens of thousands of lonely patients enjoying the longevity afforded by a society renown for its citizens' long lives but suffering from pre-senile dementia, the amiable, domesticated canines who are brought to visit them make them feel relaxed. These friendly animals can similarly build rapport with autistic children by playing with them, giving them comfort and lightening their mental anguish. Kids and elderly both benefit from a pet relaxant.

Thirdly, tame canines have a long, long history of

relationships with humans in general. According to a website called "History and Evolution of Dogs," primitive hunters first domesticated young wolf cubs ten to fifteen thousand years ago; present day dogs, in fact, evolved directly from wolves. After that, people quickly came to learn to appreciate their character, intelligence and sociability and both seemed naturally and strongly drawn to each other.

Even so, there are those who, out of love of power, desire to possess animals, especially docile, obedient and intelligent animals like dogs that want to bond, readily wagging their tail in delight at the first show of kindness or affection. The article, "Greed," in Wikipedia, The Free Encyclopedia, defines this as "the selfish desire for or pursuit of money, power, food, or other possessions ... one of the seven deadly sins." Sadly, some people seem inclined to look for someone or something loving enough to act the servant or worse, slave, simply to satisfy their greed.

To sum up, dogs, those dearest of friends, play many crucial roles in the world, especially in Japan. Because of their friendliness, helpfulness, and beneficence, dogs not only give comfort but, in some instances, become an absolute must for many patients. Without a doubt, they admirably perform the role and deserve the laudable title of most important animal and man's best friend.

How Could You Become So Big?

6

The Cruelest Animal of All

Mark Twain once said, "All war must be just the killing of strangers against whom you feel no personal animosity." How many times have humans waged bloody wars and conflicts since the dawn of history? Why can't humans stop murdering? From a historical standpoint, few would dispute the existence of human belligerence. Over the course of time, millions have massacred millions; right now, this moment, humans are killing each other somewhere in the world. Is this the only way to resolve the problem of burgeoning overpopulation and its attendant problems – to kill one another?

Historically humans have felt obliged to war when a

particular group runs short of food. Food production, however, depends largely on stability, and in times of instability like the world seems to have entered, the last refuge for food remains the oceans. To feed the starving millions and survive, humans must learn to manage and consume sea mammals, including whales and dolphins.

The founder and co-owner of Enchanted Learning Software, Jeananda Col, reported in an article called "Zoom Whales" that Sperm, Killer, Minke, Bottlenose, and Beluga whales have begun increasing in abundance. Fisheries these days must pay close attention to their numbers. The bottom line remains not only over-harvesting these kindly leviathans, but also not allowing their numbers to grow to the point of adversely impacting the reservoir of sea creatures used as food by humans.

Big eaters, these sea mammals gulp huge dinners of

krill, squid or fish, pigging out on multi-ton lunches. Reducing their numbers not only means more food for starving humans from their abundant flesh, but also more fish and other sea life, which will suddenly flourish as a result.

People also need to consider the ever-growing threat of loss of seafood from land mismanagement. As the wise saying goes, "Look to bountiful forests if you want rich fisheries." Humans should protect and foster forests. Rivers alive with nutrients bring important elements such as phosphorous, nitrogen and iron necessary for rich sea life from land to estuaries where plankton feed. People must stop over-harvesting forests, especially rainforests, in order to further stimulate fish and ocean life while carefully harvesting sea mammals. Once humans are re-established as top predators, they can proceed to eat fish and other sea animals at not just one but different trophic levels of the food chain.   Once this new balance is established, humans will have to work to preserve it.

Human population forecasts stun most people. With over 300 million in the U.S. and 6.6 billion on the globe (Population Clocks), the United Nations Food and Agriculture Organization estimated over 854 million starved worldwide in 2006 (World Hunger Facts 2008). Who would waver in their decision about which they should slaughter, a mammal or thousands of needy orphans under such impoverishing circumstances? Whaling vessels need to go out onto the oceans and rebegin catching mammals now in order to produce essential food for the hungry.

Whaling nations like Japan, with years of experience harvesting, processing and utilizing every whale body part can help. In a recent website report, the organization, Compassion on World Farming (CIWF), states that in a lifetime, an average person will consume tens of thousands of eggs, tens of thousands of gallons of milk, four beef cattle, twenty pigs, thirty sheep, forty-five turkeys, a thousand chickens, and tens of thousands of fish. One can shrug off the remark, "Over the course of my life, I have always eaten all the food served for each meal without leaving leftovers!" Actually though, people unknowingly waste thousands of pounds of scraps as well as generate hundreds of thousands of pounds of waste. Whales, however, represent not only a useful food source, and but also their byproducts, oil and bones, have commercial applications (Whales and Humans). Waste not, want not: People should make the most of every bit of this new food source.

In fact, sea mammals already face inevitable extinction. The English naturalist and geologist, Charles R. Darwin claimed in his 1859 book, <u>The Origin of Species,</u> that life naturally evolves through a process called "natural selection." In other words, Mother Nature will select and doom unfavorable species, including large-sized animals like whales, to extinction. Let the people eat whales now before they disappear on their own.

People already manage, harvest and eat many large land animals. Surf the internet for famine and starvation websites, and notice both the appallingly large number of sites and hits. I suspect that most viewers, if questioned, would respond similarly, "Sea mammals are so cute, sweet, amicable, and friendly. How could people kill whales and dolphins?" Some pet owners, on the other hand, regard poisonous snakes and spiders as adorable and cute. Can these people honestly say that they've never eaten beef, pork, chicken or hamburger? So are all these hypocrites vegan vegetarians? People need to accept that the human species, the most barbarous and atrocious animal of all, evolved this way for the specific purpose of relentlessly preying on other living things. A respected weekly science magazine recently pointed out that our "primitive" ancestors well understood this, and ate what they needed, but respectfully thanked the animals after killing them (Science News). All civilized or hungry people have to do is have the grace to thank the mammals for their sacrifice and indulge.

How many species after all have already come and gone on the earth? The International Union for the Conservation of Nature and Natural Resources (IUCN) reported, "As of September 2007, 41415 species appear on the IUCN Red List and 16306 of them are threatened with extinction" (Extinction Crisis). In the United States, the U.S. Fish and Wildlife service added that, as of May 2007, the total number of endangered species in the U.S. stood at 411 animals and 598 plants. Though scientists have a nebulous idea that habitats across the globe are losing dozens of species each day, the fundamental question still remains: does it really matter as long as there is more food for humans? No one knows exactly how many species have become extinct or have even existed on earth. Yet, even if people knew the exact number of extinct species, they could do nothing about it and furthermore, it doesn't appear to have affected the human food supply. In fact, not a single person living today has proof that changes in the earth's food chain due to extinctions have had an intrinsically bad effect on humans. On the other hand, human destruction of ecosystems for recreation, entertainment or pure profit, destruction of the lower food chain and natural resources, as well as pollution clearly do.

People must at the same time try to downsize the world's population. This along with eating sea mammals should be enough to curb or even eliminate world hunger. Before anti-whaling nations denounce whaling, they should address their own overpopulation and dog-eat-dog attitudes, all of which contribute to the exploitation of land, rivers and home waters. Humans need to start eating sea mammals just as much as they need to working to develop sustainable forestries and fisheries.

In conclusion, in order to feed the starving people of suffering countries and ultimately for humans to survive on earth, people must wake up and begin to manage, harvest and eat sea mammals – particularly whales and dolphins. Whaling countries and starving countries have to do appropriate research as they slaughter whales and dolphins for food and export them to those countries which suffer from hunger. Catching whales and dolphins to provide food for the hungry is as natural and necessary as eating land animals and being human.

Works Cited

Blatchford, John. "Whales and Humans." 18 Mar. 2008.

SUITE 101com. 25 Apr. 2008. <http://

marinebiologyoceanography.suite101.com/

article.cfm/whales_and_humans>.

Col, J. Zoom Whales. All About Whales. 2008

EnchantedLearning.com. 21 Apr. 2008. <http://

www.enchantedlearning.com/subjects/whales/>.

"Charles Darwin." WikipediA, The Free Encyclopedia.

26 Apr. 2008. Wikimedia Foundation, Inc. 26 Apr.

2008. <http://en.wikipedia.org/wiki/

Charles_Darwin>.

CIWF. Food Chains and Farm animals. Downloaded 21

Apr. 2008. <http://ciwf.org/publications/Teachers/

SW/SCI_FoodChain.pdf>.

"Extinction crisis escalates: Red List shows apes,

corals, vultures, dolphins all in danger." The IUCN

Species Survival Commission. 22 Apr. 2008.

<http://www.iucnredlist.org/>.

"Mark Twain." <u>WikipediA, The Free Encyclopedia</u>. 16

Apr. 2008. Wikimedia Foundation, Inc. 18 Apr.

2008. <http://en.wikipedia.org/wiki/Mark_Twain>.

"New Technology Shows Our ancestors Ate…

Everything!" Science Daily. Retrieved April 30,

2008. 26 Apr. 2008. <http://www.sciencedaily.com/

releases/2005/08/050805111026.htm>.

U.S. Census Bureau. "U.S. and World Population

Clocks – POPClocks." 22 November, 2006. U.S.

Census Bureau, Population Division. 21 Apr. 2008

<http://www.census.gov/main/www/

popclock.html>.

World Hunger Education service. "World Hunger Facts

2008." Updated Mar. 1 2008. 21 Apr. 2008.

<http://www.worldhunger.org/articles/Learn/

<u>world%20hunger%20facts%202002.htm</u>>.

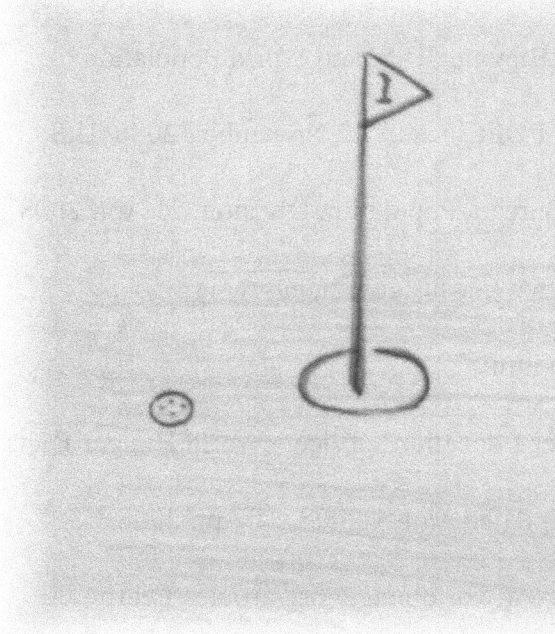

A Tough Putt to Drop

7

As White As Snow

Observers wowed as the small object arched high and long through the open sky. Hundreds of inquisitive eyes watched as it rolled to a stop several hundred yards away.

At first glance, this object has a completely smooth spherical body - a full moon face as white as snow. On closer examination, however, the more astute will recognize, not pimples, but about 400 dimples in orderly sequence all over its scarred face.

Weighing in at about one point six ounces, with a diameter of roughly one point seven inches, a branded name and number appears on each side of its chubby face.

According to Wikipedia, The Free Encyclopedia, it all started in 1550, when a Scottish dilettante made a wooden one.   Later, people tightly packed goose feathers into a cowhide pouch.   More recently, a number made from tree sap, appeared on the market, quickly followed by modern multi-layer ones, built of a wide variety of synthetic materials like, for instance, urethane.

Outside this object is almost always surrounded by a tough, almost crystal-hard flack-jacket.   A healthy, adult pitbull with its strong jaws and sharp incisor teeth would leave only tiny teeth marks in its surface. People, on the other hand, if they wanted to, could barely get it into their mouths, much less leave any mark on its shiny surface.   Though generally odorless and tasteless, if its hard shell is pierced or it comes new out of a box, it can smell sharp and rubbery and taste bitter.

If it hits concrete or asphalt, it bounces back high, with a sharp crack.

A last hint: Its snow-white-full-moon face makes it conspicuously present when on the green.

My Image of London

<u>8</u>

I Remember It All Very Clearly

After spending several years working part-time for a furniture company, Yasu saved enough money to purchase a discounted air ticket to Heathrow. "I did it!" he yelled, jumping up and down. A new chapter in his life dawned that spring day thirty years ago.

Once a long time ago, a friend of a friend, Hiroyuki, had visited England and returned to Japan with one wondrously exotic tale after another. Hiroyuki had also told Yasu about a Mr. Onishi who currently lived in England.

At last the big day arrived. Saying good-bye to his family, the young man got on board a Korean Air Lines plane. The aircraft roared, trembled uncontrollably, and sped down the runway. The force of the airplane pressed him back against the seat as hundreds of tons of solid metal took off like a paper plane up into the sky. Holding tightly onto the arms of his seat, his fingers and thumbs turning white, the whirring sound of the aircraft and the rumble of the wheels folding into belly of the airplane shook him up. He could almost imagine reaching out and touching the sky but luckily was too petrified to try.

After twenty four hours, however, the thrilling newness of flying had worn off, and in a stupor, this London newcomer dragged his body out of the plane and through customs. Almost everything new and exciting that he had vowed never to forget during that interminably long flight slipped from his memory.

Outside the Heathrow airport terminal, a taxi approached and the driver offered to drive him to his friend, Mr. Onishi's flat in London proper. Alas, after more than an hour and a half, Yasu still had not arrived at the elusive Mr. Onishi's. The driver mumbled, holding the piece of paper with Mr. Onishi's address on it first right side up, then upside down with a quizzical look on his face. The cabby's murmuring perturbed him; sadly, though, everything the driver said completely eluded him. Eventually the taxi stopped in front of a police station and the driver asked for help. To this day Yasu could only remember bits and pieces of the conversation: "Where on earth ... too many roads ... same name ... enormous taxi fare!" The policeman must have given the driver a clue; the taxi finally rolled to a stop in front of Mr. Onishi's flat on the East End where many expatriates lived.

While knocking on the huge wood door, he luckily noticed Mr. Onishi exiting a side door for school; the hardworking student had mistaken Yasu's arrival date for the following day.

Mr. Onishi kindly suggested Yasu stay in the flat until school finished in the afternoon. Almost instantly, Yasu fell fast asleep, waking up when his new friend returned.   That afternoon, Mr. Onishi found his Japanese guest a B&B (bed-and-breakfast) hotel nearby, and the two ate out together.

That night Yasu said good night to the B&B landlord, dashed straight to bed, and slept like a log. He awoke the next evening and he blurted out his first complete English sentence: "Hello, my name is Yasuo Kobachi," to the landlord, who, it turns out, had worried all night about what had happened to his guest. Feeling once again like a million bucks, Yasu rejoiced, "I've broken all my old sleeping records."   And so began Yasu's first day in England. I remember it all very clearly. I'm Yasu. I visited London and, like Hiroyuki, had many wondrously exotic adventures I'd like to tell you about the next time we meet.

A Peaceful Beach at the Meeting Place

9

The Story of Foteatupolit, Heat

T. Gas, and Flood A. Drought

Once upon a time in a galaxy far, far away, there existed a cozy, mostly tropical planet called, oddly enough, "Earth." This Earth sported six large continents divided between its Northern and Southern Hemispheres, and a variety of animate beings inhabited the lands.

Three invincible golfers in particular lived there roaming at large. Their names: Forteatupolit, Heat T. Gas, and Flood A. Drought. Their skills were such that no one could match them, and the three never vied for the top in any tournament together, because that game of games would simply never have ended.

One day on a balmy spring afternoon, chance led them to meet at a restaurant in town.   There they chatted amicably about friends and tournaments.

"Why don't we play together next Sunday, not for competition, but just for fun?" one player casually remarked.

"Great idea!" said the others, satisfied with the proposal.

On Sunday the three golfers met on the first tee ground at Wikiwaki Golf Links, a particularly well-kept golf course located in the exact center of the planet, to start the game.   One player tossed a coin to choose who would play first.   The privilege of teeing off first went to the medium built man from Notame continent named Forteatupolit.

"Hurrah!" people from the gallery, probably friends of his, cheered.

This first player, Forteatupolit, belonged to a new

anthropoid race called Hominids, and in those days, two types of Hominids resided on the land; Goofy Saps and Good Citizens. Unfortunately, the Goofy Saps dominated the land, and the majority of innocent Good Citizens had to bow down to their bigger Goofy Sap masters who, in turn, had to bow down to handful of particularly affluent, mercenary politicos of whom, to keep this story short, we shall not speak. The continent, Notame, always elected its head politicos, and the Hominids there had overwhelmingly voted in Forteatupolit and his ilk.

Forteatupolit, steeped in evil, received a lion's share of all national business under his notorious bureaucracy. In fact, he had a penchant for fooling other fellow Hominids on the continent. A militant surrounded by potent lobbyists quite willing to bribe any Hominids he asked them to, he sought to increase military expenditures at the expense of efforts against global warming, his number one priority to abandon his continent's economy to line his own pockets. Forteatupolit closed his mind to all Good Citizens' appeals, such as reducing greenhouse gases. Sad to say, Hominids chose him a second time as well.

The second golfer looked like a supernatural phantom and came from a different continent from the other two. "That's a beauty!" the crowd roared loudly and condescendingly as she teed off.

Many Hominids disliked her grumpy, cranky and moody personality. She afflicted all animate things on planet Earth, whenever she raged against the antipathetic Hominids. Her super power, namely dehydrating then deluging, often ended up swamping and even washing away the houses of Hominids everywhere on the continents, terrorizing them. Sometimes she relentlessly attacked the farmlands of the innocent by drying out the vegetation. Good

Citizens tried as hard as they could to identify what triggered her violent outbursts but once she started, they had to watch helplessly as she wreaked her havoc. Hominids gave her the name of Flood A. Drought. No Hominid knew where she came from or what she wanted.

Heat T. Gas, the biggest of the group, waved to the visitors in a friendly manner. He had come from nowhere to become something. He also had a mystic force. He could wrap around everything on land and keep everything warm, melting down even gigantic blocks of sea ice. His ability seemed to increase year by year, which caused fear and consternation among Good Citizens. Just like his invisible figure, the animate beings could not spot where the golf ball he drove went.

Forteatupolit, Heat T. Gas, and Flood A. Drought ruled over the Earth with the help of the Goofy Saps for a long time. They kept winning until the land came to doomsday.

At the eleventh hour, the underdog Good Citizens finally stood up against them. They overthrew the evil government and chose not Forteatupolit, but a man named Civil Servant from among the Good Citizens. Forteatupolit had apparently passed his prime as a golfer anyway. Civil Servant tried to indoctrinate the Hominids on how to create an ideal democracy for Earth. Gradually, the Hominids came to realize that only science could work out the problems that science produced. With Civil Servant's assistance Hominids brought together rational, sensible scientists from all over the Earth. Through the process of trial and error, they eventually found the best way to break free from the bed of thorns the silly Hominids had created. Heat T. Gas and Flood A. Drought, hearing this, slowly drifted away and the Hominids, having turned over a new leaf, looked towards a happy future.

Have Some Healthy Tropical Drink!

10

Imposition of an Overweight

Tax on the Overweight

No one cares about what overweight people eat, even less their physical activities or myriad obesity factors, but as long as they want to live in a community, they have to take some responsibility for the inconvenience and trouble they cause. For theirs and everyone else's benefit, governments should impose an overweight tax on overweight people.

Certainly some people of average height and weight have sighed at their misfortune when sandwiched between two colossal guys or blocked from watching a movie. Some people may have even gone through the discomfort of sharing an elevator with a plump, round woman, who, breathlessly, seemed to draw in all the oxygen in the elevator only to make everybody else choke to death. Others, though they had urgent work to do, may have had to give up getting on the elevator, thanks to one 350-pound passenger. Has anyone seen an overweight bus passenger hogging two seats during a two-for-one fare special? Overweight people have the same legitimate rights to public facilities but should pay extra charges or, better yet, an overweight tax.

Overweight individuals, having no basic manners, often offend others. At 11:30 a.m. on March 9, 2008, a party of four teed off at Ko Olina Golf Club in Hawaii. One Japanese visitor and three local Hawaii friends were playing together until a two-player group ahead of them suddenly disappeared. The four golfers thought the two guys, one thin in yellow and one grossly obese in blue respectively had finished the hole, so the Japanese visitor got ready to hit a driver. All three local golfers simultaneously yelled, "Oh, shoot!" when they spotted the elephantine guy in blue swinging a club in the bush. No one could imagine how a party of only two stuck players could keep all the parties behind waiting! Looking exactly like an ad balloon, the man in blue could not move easily, shuffled along and, even worse, the two guys' slow play showed no spirit. After some time, an impatient two-people party behind the four asked if they would let the two through. However, yellow and blue had, in the meantime, damaged the green with their spiked soles so badly that the four shouted, "Where are those lead-footed guys' manners?" In the scorecard they had noticed rules saying, "Proper golf attire and etiquette is required at all times. Please avoid slow play by keeping pace with the group in front." Clearly if the state had levied an overweight tax on all overweight players this situation might never have occurred.

Airlines should follow suit! It simply doesn't make sense not to! For example, in March 2007, a Japanese student at Intercultural Communications College (ICC) in Hawaii went to the Honolulu Airport to return home. Near the United Airlines' counter, he witnessed a tourist couple checking their luggage. An attendant lifted the luggage and put it on a scale, saying, "We must charge you extra because this is overweight." Feeling sorry for them, the student nonetheless went through the security check. Unluckily he ended up sitting on the plane next to a huge guy. How come airlines don't seem to know the difference between a pound of a suitcase and a pound of human fat? Why doesn't the government require overweight people like those with overweight baggage to pay extra?

Humongous people have to keep in mind the fact that the heavier a burden a vehicle has, the more fuel it guzzles. Obese people, who are more likely to own a big SUV, van or pickup truck, waste much more precious gas than thin people. According to the Analysis Blog for Measures to Improve Fuel Economy at http://nenpi1.com, when a heavy driver sits in a car, the "rolling resistance" of the tires increases, which makes the car get worse gas mileage, resulting in a 10 to 20% loss in fuel economy of a car. Similarly, a research group at Illinois University reported at http://air.ap.teacup.com/spirit/214.html that based on an estimated 223,000,000 American cars, if every car in America gained one pound, they would consume 39,000,000 gallons more of gas a year. The taxation system in America does not do justice to overweight people. The heavier the load gets, the more costly the world becomes. Someone's got to pay. It should be the obese who cause the problem in the first place!

To sum it all up, the government simply must impose an overweight tax on overweight people in order to pay for their added expense. Obese people should also realize that they often offend the feelings of others and should take responsibility for the inconvenience and trouble they cause. Everyone including the obese must not allow such injustices to exist and should demand that government pass and enforce social sanctions against heavy people for both the breach of etiquette and for the precious energy loss they inflict.

Been There, Done That

11

Brave New World

Continental Airlines flight 14 departed just a few minutes behind schedule from Honolulu International Airport. To Yasu, an Intercultural Communications College (ICC) student from Japan, and self-proclaimed captain of a group of pilgrims leaving everything familiarly oriental behind, an adventure unlike any he had ever experienced had begun.

The nine-and-a-half-hour flight brought him, his brother, Mitsu, and his sister, Michi, to where the first immigrants landed in the New World. However, when these three tired explorers stepped out of the terminal building at Newark Airport, no friendly, feathered natives were waiting to greet them with Thanksgiving dinner. Instead, lost in a frenzied mob of faceless, rushing people, he immediately had to face his first challenge: catching a cab. The sticky, sultry air engulfed the three excursionists. Unknown to them their embarkation had made history: the temperature that day, 99 degrees Fahrenheit, an all-time record high for New York in the early summer, made the front page news.

At the taxi stand, a lady taxi attendant asked the three dazed siblings from Hawaii their destination and gave them a sheet of paper listing various taxi fares to various, exotic-sounding destinations. The detailed fare schedule so impressed the leader that he and his entourage hopped in, showing the cab driver in turn a piece of paper with their hotel's name and address on it. The four happily chewed the fat on the way, the driver speaking in what they later decided must have been broken Bengalese and the adventurers answering in the most respectful Japanese they could muster from their tired brains. The taxi driver never forgot to smile back at the three siblings even when it became apparent to all that it was taking considerable extra time to reach the hotel in Mid Town. To tell the truth, the driver's smiles surprised and delighted them because his group had rarely seen dark-skinned people in the Pacific Rim where they were from and fewer yet with a smile.

After riding through what seemed to them to be most of the Big Apple, when the taxi finally stopped, their first impression was that their driver had inadvertently taken them to the wrong address. Their expensive hotel looked old and dilapidated, the area dirty and messy. The three new New Yorkers had arrived at Seventh Avenue, one of the busiest streets in Manhattan. Quickly readjusting their expectations, they asked the hotel receptionist to keep their baggage while they met with their travel agent headquartered only a few blocks away.   After copious reassurances by the

agent that their hotel was, indeed, everything promised

– a prince in peasant garb so to speak - the three

checked in and settled down in their fifth floor room.

Exhausted, they grabbed an hour of sleep and upon

awakening ordered some sandwiches and beer – the

first food in New York City.   Satisfied at last, they

walked to the ground floor of the Pennsylvania (Penn)

Station just across from their well-disguised four-star

hotel.   Yasu stood and stared, awestruck at the

constantly moving, shoulder to shoulder mass of non-

orientals. He had never seen so many, doing so much,

in the same place, at the same time. After 15 minutes,

their excitement already wearing thin, they returned to

their hotel and slept away the rest of their first night in

New York.

Early next morning, three, eager beavers, stood in

the lobby of their hotel looking for the tour guide who

would take them back to Penn Station and assist them onto an Amtrak train to Boston. Once on Amtrak, the three took their seats and rode four hours, arriving at Boston, where they met another guide. This one showed them around "Bean Town," including a wonderful old park called the Boston Common, where Bostonians of old heard and discussed the latest news, and Faneuil Hall Market Place, where the elderly shopped and savored Boston's specialty clam chowder. From there, they traveled to Beacon Hill, where many English-Americans had and, according to the travel guide, still lived. The Hill, a high-end residential area, with three-storied rows of red-brick town houses built along narrow, gaslit cobblestone lanes redolent of a nostalgic cinema scene, lined up at rigid attention. His brother and sister especially liked these archaic, venerable residences.

The three then dropped by the Massachusetts

Institute of Technology (MIT) to critically examine the latest in American restroom technology. The razor-sharp ICC student, always on the lookout for something interesting, immediately noticed something wrong with the carved letters on the façade of their edifice. The letter "u" in "Massachusetts" and "Institute" had been erroneously replaced with a "v!" After vociferously pointing this out to the guide, their smiling escort explained courteously, "In early days, that was a popular trend." After satisfying their curiosity over this apparently intentional mistake, their guide took them on to Fenway Park, the home-field of the Boston Red Sox, and though unplanned, past a small sidestreet named "Dais-k" after a Japanese major leaguer (Daisuke Matsuzaka). Here was something the Japanese group could, at last, bite their teeth into, and they gracefully acknowledged America's magnanimity towards other cultures that shared greater human interests, like baseball. Before taking the return train to NYC, the three sampled Samuel Adams beer, which the guide insisted was an essential part of experiencing the history of Boston. The three drank gratifyingly and that night slept soundly back at their NYC designer hotel.

The next day, the three adventurers got together with other tourists to take a sightseeing trip around the Big Apple. They gaped respectfully at United Nations Headquarters, Trump Towers, Ground 0 and the Statue of Liberty on Liberty Island. A shout from a ferry attendant at the pier, "Keep moving. Don't stop on the gangway!" intrigued Yasu while he boarded the boat for Liberty Island.

He, in spite of himself, asked his neighbor, "'Where's the 'gang?' Are they really coming this way?" After the day-long walking tour in the city, the three took a short break in their hotel room and an early dinner at a Japanese restaurant which one of the guides recommended. At the restaurant, they enjoyed a brief respite from everything New York and soaked up the sedate, placid Japanese atmosphere, recharging their batteries for the next exciting day to come.

At 3:30 a.m. the three New Yorkers woke up to get ready to go to Canada. Luckily they only had to shuffle sleepily downstairs to their hotel lobby meeting place. This time, a driver and guide took them and five other visitors to the John F. Kennedy (JFK) Airport to fly to a local airport – Buffalo – on the outskirts of New York State and to meet another guide who would take them across a bridge spanning the border river between America and Canada and into the great unknown Canadian wilderness. All eight tourists cleared Customs, though the student's brother had a little trouble with his passport because he had brought two passports (one extra for emergencies he said) and had showed the wrong one. After rather easily convincing

Canadian officials that he was not James Bond travelling incógnito, the group happily set out to see one of the world-famous natural wonders of the world.

They looked over Niagara Falls from three different angles, put on rain coats and boarded a river boat that came close enough to the falls to splash them with spray after spray of icy-cold water. The green color of the waterfalls especially fascinated his sister. The three enjoyed magnificent vistas in Canada and a great lunch at a hotel overlooking the Falls. After buying some gifts for friends at a nearby country store, they caught what their friendly guide told them was the next "regularly scheduled delayed return flight" to JFK.

At JFK, however, something disquieting happened to their trusty Jet Blue. The pilots would not move the plane an inch after landing. The captain of the jet finally announced that there was something wrong with its communication system, at least that's what they thought. After nearly an hour, the captain reluctantly added that something also appeared wrong with its brakes. Some time later, an airport truck with emergency lights flashing approached the jet to tow it to the terminal. This time the captain had to apologize to the passengers for a malfunction in the boarding bridge, and everyone on board, sick of hearing excuses, booed all at once. One disembarking passenger grumbled that he at last understood how airlines in America made their profit. Arriving late at the hotel, the exhausted three compromised between American, Japanese and Canadian cuisine by going to a Chinese buffet for dinner.

The next, and admittedly worst day of their trip, the three shoppers slept in and consequently had to jog 30 minutes to their group meeting place at a not-so-nearby-as-they-thought Hilton Hotel. There they each grabbed a small take-out breakfast before getting into an already hot and crowded van with six other determined outlet shoppers and began a day of rushed shopping in the suburbs of the Big Apple. The inveterate shoppers dragged the poor ICC student from store to store until his legs hurt and the bottoms of his feet got sore. The women of the group seemed to have an insatiable propensity for shopping. Even though his sister's legs clearly felt like stones, she still wanted to look at more brand-name goods. Despite their best efforts, the three siblings from Hawaii still weren't able to visit all the stores and buy out all of the amazing bargain goods within the vast outlet complex. The leader pointed out to no avail that many of the shops looked amazingly like those of the same name in Hawaii.

The next day was decidedly better. The three unanimously decided that it was time to become Washingtonians. Now able to read the Amtrak information (timetable) on the TV monitor at the Penn

Station, they joined four other people for a day trip to the nation's capital. In spite of their new found ability, however, they discovered a friendly guide waiting for them at Union Station.

The group visited, in quick succession, the White House, Capitol Hill, Arlington National Cemetery, and what proved the most popular sightseeing spot, the National Air and Space Museum (NASM). In the process, the three learned that the word, DC, stood for District of Columbia. The District of Columbia was, they discovered, not a state at all but rather an independent territory. The adventurous trio then explored the territory, in the process meeting Lincoln, viewing his famous emancipation speech and standing on the stone pavement where Martin Luther King Jr. delivered his famous "I have a Dream" speech before 200,000 cheering Americans. While Yasu's brother and sister took a break at a small restaurant, the ICC student ran to the Smithsonian, a stately building nearby, where for a short while and at no charge he paid his respects to some of his favorite post-impressionist artists. Then he learned that the museum allowed visitors to take pictures of even the greatest works. He immediately began innocently taking one after another flash photograph, until an attendant rushed to his side and politely but firmly warned him not to use a flash. He apologized profusely, but at the same time, couldn't help but enjoy having these treasures to the public!

Rejoining the group, he got a final peek at more stately, majestic architectural treasures. Although the return train to NYC proved rather crowded, they remained ease when they found that tickets holders had reserved seats. Sensible enough. There couldn't be too much more than 100 % congestion that way. Nevertheless, during the three-and-a-half-hour ride, the three Washingtonians from Hawaii eventually got fed up with two Americans who couldn't stop chitchatting on their cell phones. The three concluded irritably that that seemed very American though.

The next day, a rest day, the three had no scheduled plan, so they decided to window shop on Fifth Avenue until, once again, their legs got tired and they stopped for a prix fixe lunch at a department store. Who said there was no inexpensive food in New York?

The next day, the three much older feeling folks ventured to take their first subway ride all by themselves. Checking which train would take them to their destination of the day, they walked down into the entrance, making sure they found the right track by repeatedly asking a station attendant. Suddenly they noticed that two types of ticket machines stood between them and their track, so like a fearless native yours truly stepped forward and asked a lady in line if the machine she was waiting for could sell a single ride ticket – a two-dollar ticket used only once without transferring to a bus. She answered in the affirmative, but try as they might, the three musketeers could not get the wary machine to give up its treasure. Thinking of who he should question next, he finally cornered a family group that looked new to the subway, battling more successfully with another ticket machine. Valiant to the last, he told his brother and sister to wait at the side and watch the locals purchase tickets while he tried once again to wrest the necessary secret information from the station attendant. After a few minutes, the two observers beckoned him back. Pooling their information together, they finally got three metro-cards. They then slipped the cards through the indicated slot like a credit card, pushed the turnstile and moved forward to the platform. Their reward: a shabby, dim, crowded area that nonetheless graffiti-free appeared less threatening than it might have. The low roof of the subway, however, soon induced in him a claustrophobic feeling.

In a wink, the train appeared and they hit the road getting off at the 86th Street station at the West side of Central Park. As they climbed the steps up to Central Park, one of his group anonymously mentioned that interestingly, riding the train took much less time than purchasing the tickets.

Map in hand but still confused by the maze of walkways around the Metropolitan Museum, it proved difficult for him to relax and enjoy the spacious green lawn. Even with the map, he still ended up needing to ask one passerby after another for help.

The three made it through the park at last and shuffled up to the ticket counter of the museum. Once again, they saw everything they wanted to, but only with the assistance of the many kindly museum attendants and viewers.

Worn-out from walking, the trio grabbed a cab in front of the museum and sped off to a – yes, you guessed it – Japanese restaurant recommended by one of their tour guides. Little did they know that this dinner engagement included pre-dinner entertainment: As the driver pulled out and started the meter, another cab broadsided them! The three watched in awe the American drama that subsequently unfolded before their eyes. Their free three-minute Broadway play proved interesting and entertaining. Though just a fender bender, the two drivers complained to each other in rapid-fire English, blaming each other for every catastrophe since World War Two but in the end, agreeing with collusive smiles not to call the police. After the play, the three savored a better lunch than even their friends in Hawaii. Happily the food in New York continued to prove less expensive than Hawaii except at the fanciest restaurants.

The three now avid New Yorkers strolled along Seventh Avenue to try a new distinctly American culinary challenge - the Red Lobster Restaurant - for their final evening. They had heard from their guide in Bean Town that the best seafood in NYC came from Boston and the Red Lobster, everyone said, served the best Boston seafood.

Once there and duly seated, a waitress took their drink orders and a long time to serve their meals. Eventually a cook in white came to their table, holding plates of whole red lobsters and shrimps, asking if all the orders had come, but he spoke so fast in what seemed like an entirely new language, that the threesome simply smiled and nodded politely. Actually, they were still awaiting their appetizers which had still not come yet.

At 7:30 p.m., fat with Boston lobster, they checked in at the Minskoff Theatre for a Broadway play they had purchased tickets for.   Unfortunately, they arrived too early to be seated.   Eventually, however, everyone found a seat.   By eight, curtain time, the house was packed.   Suddenly the lights dimmed, the curtain rose and an actress began singing on the stage along with two actors in the mezzanine, a breathtaking twist that got the author hook, line and sinker.   The student from Hawaii could not resist leaning forward to gaze at every fabulous detail as though he understood every word. New York musicals, the three agreed, deserved their reputation.   For the next couple hours, they discussed every prop and song, even venturing in the process several good guesses as to what musical they had just seen.

Intoxicated with delight, the three New Yorkers merrily walked back to their hotel along brightly-lit Seventh Avenue, speaking words of praise for the show and their overall wonderful excursion to the Big Apple.

Even back home in Hawaii, happy as a clam, the transitory New Yorkers kept repeating, "Yoka-tta (great!)," after quickly running out of American adjectives equal to their great experience.

Looking back, the ICC student liked the last night's show all the more for his successful struggle buying the tickets online.   His brother felt pleased particularly because everything went off without a hitch; amazing, since being a sort of blasé person, he didn't get excited often.   His sister admired New Yorkers' sophistication for always appearing crisp, neat and clean, despite the challenges of living in a big city life.   She loved lively New York, and especially enjoyed the vibrant excitement in the air.   In the end, the author most enjoyed remembering the large number of good, friendly and hospitable Americans, which caused him to alter an earlier more one-sided view about them, especially the big city dwellers.

At the red lobster restaurant, a young waitress readily responded to Yasu's request for a Band Aid when he cut his finger in the lobster's pincher. In the Empire State Building, curious about the age of the building, he had successfully talked with a lady, probably from another state. She willingly chatted with him and even went so far as to make reference to an extra charge the visitors would have to pay if they wanted to go up higher than 86th floor of the building, very thoughtful of her. Another time, when he had gone over to Minskoff to confirm the place and time of their Lion King show, he caught sight of a theater attendant busily serving a long line of waiting theater-goers. He had intrepidly asked the attendant for help, not realizing he had the wrong theatre. The attendant, even in such a hectic situation, kindly helped him.

This ICC student couldn't even give a ballpark figure as to how many walkers and joggers at Central

Park he had had to rely on, for example, to visit the Metropolitan Museum where for a while the three completely lost wanderers almost thought they might have to just stay for the night. The wonderfully genuine New Yorkers, however, never abandoned them. One thing the three friends agreed on most: they had at last come to like and apreciate these amicable Americans.

About the Author

Yasuo Kobachi was born in Japan and taught English and Japanese at a private school for 25 years. He is currently staying in the USA and excited about sharing his experiences with others.

If you enjoyed *Essay, Essay, Essay,* consider these other fine books from Savant Books and Publications:

Aloha from Coffee Island by Walter Miyanari
Footprints, Smiles and Little White Lies by Daniel S. Janik
The Illustrated Middle Earth by Daniel S. Janik
Last and Final Harvest by Daniel s. Janik
A Whale's Tale by Daniel S. Janik
Tropic of California by R. Page Kaufman
Tropic of California (the companion music CD) by R. Page Kaufman
The Village Curtain by Tony Tame
Dare to Love in Oz by William Maltese
The Interzone by Tatsuyuki Kobayashi
Today I Am a Man by Larry Rodness
The Bahrain Conspiracy by Bentley Gates
Called Home by Gloria Schumann
Kanaka Blues by Mike Farris
First Breath edited by Z. M. Oliver
Poor Rich by Jean Blasiar
The Jumper Chronicles - Quest for Merlin's Map by W. C. Peever
William Maltese's Flicker by William Maltese
My Unborn Child by Orest Stocco
Last Song of the Whales by Four Arrows
Perilous Panacea by Ronald Klueh
Falling but Fulfilled by Zachary M. Oliver
Mythical Voyage by Robin Ymer
Hello, Norma Jean by Sue Dolleris
Richer by Jean Blasiar
Manifest Intent by Mike Farris
Charlie No Face by David B. Seaburn
Number One Bestseller by Brian Morley
My Two Wives and Three Husbands by S. Stanley Gordon
In Dire Straits by Jim Currie
Wretched Land by Mila Komarnisky
Chan Kim by Ilan Herman
Who's Killing All the Lawyers? by A. G. Hayes
Ammon's Horn by G. Amati
Wavelengths edited by Zachary M. Oliver
Almost Paradise by Laurie Hanan

Communion by Jean Blasiar and Jonathan Marcantoni
The Oil Man by Leon Puissegur
Random Views of Asia from the Mid-Pacific by William E. Sharp
The Isla Vista Crucible by Reilly Ridgell
Blood Money by Scott Mastro
In the Himalayan Nights by Anoop Chandola
Rules of Privilege by Mike Farris
On My Behalf by Helen Doan
Fifty-Eight Stones edited by Daniel S. Janik
Light Surfer by David Allan Williams
Traveler's Rest by Jonathan Marcantoni
Keys in the River by Tendai Mwanaka
The Path of the Templar by W. C. Peever
The Loons by Sue Dolleris
The Judas List by A. G. Hayes
Path of the Templar - The Jumper Chronicles Book II by W. C. Peever
The Desperate Cycle by Tony Tame

Coming Works:
Shutterbug by Buz Sawyers
Blessed are the Peacekeepers by Tom Donnelly and Mike Munger
The Lazarus Conspiracies by Richard Rose

http://www.savantbooksandpublications.com

www.ingramcontent.com/pod-product-compliance
Lightning Source LLC
Chambersburg PA
CBHW072010170626
46813CB00005B/2103